WHO WAS THIS BUKHARIN?

Who was this Bukharin?

KEN COATES

SPOKESMAN

First published in 2011 by
Spokesman
Russell House
Bulwell Lane, Nottingham NG6 0BT, England
Phone 0115 9708318
Fax 0115 9420433
e-mail elfeuro@compuserve.com
www.spokesmanbooks.com

Copyright © Ken Coates 2010

All rights reserved. No part of this publication may be reproduced, stored in a retrieval system or transmitted in any form or by any means electronic, mechanical, photocopying, recording or otherwise, without the prior permission of the publishers.

ISBN13: 978-0-85124 7816

A CIP Catalogue record is available from the British Library

Printed by the Russell Press Ltd.
(phone 0115 9784505 www.russellpress.com)

CONTENTS

1 Who was this Bukharin? 7

2 Bukharin's testament 37

2 Bukharin's letter to Stalin 41

4 Interview with Yuri Larin, Bukharin's son 53

Stalin, Rykov (in dark suit), and Bukharin leading the funeral procession for Felix Dzerzhinsky in Red Square, 1926.

1
Who was this Bukharin?

Late in the Spring of 1978 I received a letter from Yuri Larin. It was sent on to me by the Russian historian, Roy Medvedev, in the hope that I might be able to help secure a response.

Larin, a painter, was the son of the one-time Soviet leader, Nikolai Bukharin. Bukharin was the youngest of the senior leaders of the Russian October Revolution, sometimes described in the earliest days of 1917 as Lenin's favourite. He had been judicially murdered after a grisly show trial which marked the culmination of Stalin's round of purges in the late thirties, and Larin was trying to secure his father's rehabilitation. Who was this Bukharin?

> 'If Lenin represented the first revolutionary generation of Bolsheviks and Trotsky the second, Bukharin belonged to the third – he was only in his thirties when I first met him,'

wrote Joseph Berger, an early secretary of the Palestine Communist Party.

> 'Of all the Politbureau, he had been the one who disagreed and argued with Lenin most often.

They complemented each other, and their differences gave life and movement to the intellectual leadership. But he regarded himself as Lenin's pupil and imitated his manners, his resolute air and his crisp, dramatically simple way of expressing himself. It was the fashion, set by Lenin, to reduce the most involved political and philosophical notions to the simplest formulas. However, Bukharin's ideas were less clear cut, he was less shrewdly aware of their practical implications, and he relied more on brilliance of style.

It was said afterwards, when the hunt was up, that he was too dogmatic. His books may support this view, but in conversation he was warm, flexible and impressionable. He digressed freely, and you could feel that he was talking partly to make up his own mind. He was interested in what other people had to say. He drew out his subordinates, and never let them feel snubbed when a decision went against them. He surrounded himself with young people and students. They liked him and he influenced their ideas (for a time this was useful to Stalin, who had none of his expansive charm).[1]

In 1938, Bukharin burst into the headlines of Western newspapers as the principal accused in the third of the great purge trials in Moscow. As a result of these trials, Stalin rid himself of all the most celebrated revolutionary leaders, and consolidated his position as the absolute ruler of the Soviet Union. The trials were all marked by grotesque features, the most notable of which was that the accused outdid one another in their determination to admit to the most lurid and preposterous charges.

The three major trials took place in August 1936, January 1937, and finally in March 1938. There were other lesser processes, and many people were simply arbitrarily dispatched without any kind of public hearing.

All these proceedings were directed, *in absentia*, against Leon Trotsky, who was accused of fostering conspiracies of a widely divergent group of people, including former Soviet Prime Ministers and distinguished political spokesmen. All the participants in these trials 'confessed' to a wide variety of acts of sabotage, terror and treason. All claimed to be the employees of different intelligence services or the hirelings of foreign states. None of these claims have subsequently been validated. When the post-war Nuremburg War Crimes Tribunal was asked by H. G. Wells and other writers to report upon the allegations in the Moscow Trials about complicity between the Moscow accused and the Hitler Government, this issue was decisively avoided.

The trials were the public face of a major trauma which followed a change of policy by Stalin in 1929. Up to that time, he had been in a close alliance with Bukharin to ensure the maintenance of a 'new economic policy' initiated by Lenin, which sought to manage policies towards the peasantry in a conciliatory fashion. Trotsky stood apart from this consensus, and led an opposition which argued for more rapid industrial development and an attempt to gradually extend the collective ownership and management of farms by consent, alongside the accelerated mechanisation of agriculture.

A fierce dilemma arose in 1929, with the world-wide economic crisis, when Stalin broke with Bukharin and his policies, initiating both a radical speed-up in industrial development, and a policy of breakneck forced collectivisation on the land. This caused serious divisions in Trotsky's left opposition, since it could be argued that Stalin had now taken over a major part of the opposition's programme. Successive sections of Trotsky's following were to split away to make their peace with Stalin or, at any rate, to seek to reintegrate themselves in the Communist Party. Isaac Deutscher has described this process in some detail. It undoubtedly brought some of the most talented of Trotsky's original followers back into the official fold, albeit with various degrees of reluctance and often serious reservations. None of these people were thenceforward given major political responsibilities, but some of them were found very demanding technical jobs, or an important role in economic administration.

There were different types of reconciliation. Some leaders such as Radek made their peace and roundly denounced Trotsky. On the other hand, later attempts at reconciliation were made by groups which refused to renounce Trotsky, or which actually demanded the ending of his exile and his readmission to the political process.

In April 1929, Preobrazhensky tried to bring all the 'conciliators' together with an appeal 'to all comrades in opposition!' While it suited Stalin to encourage the defection of Trotsky's closest supporters, he had no intention of accepting their claim that the change in Soviet policy represented a victory for the ideas of that opposition. Held at arms length, Preobrazhensky did not succeed in uniting 'all the comrades of the opposition', and the result was a succession of different capitulations, leaving only a fraction of the original opposition unreconciled and irreconcilable.

These various capitulators were to form a substantial part of the *dramatis personae* of the Moscow trials.

But if the Trotskyist opposition found itself embroiled in serious difficulties as a result of the abrupt change of policy by Stalin, there was a delayed action outbreak of problems for Stalin himself. Did, in fact, the change of policy entail a belated recognition of the justice in the opposition's earlier programme? The brutal conduct of collectivisation went far beyond the recommendations originally made by Trotsky, and amounted to a declaration of war on a substantial part of the peasantry. This generated severe social tensions, and culminated in the outbreak of famine. These were, indeed, horrendous times for all the Communists, not only the oppositionists. They entailed elaborate crises of conscience, and fierce political convulsions. At the climax of this turmoil, the opposition found themselves actually on trial for their lives, indicted alongside their inveterate opponents, Bukharin and his closest intimates. These included former Premier Rykov, who had been an architect of the very policies to which the opposition had originally objected, and was now paraded as a significant section of the unmasked opposition to Stalin. None were simply accused of political dissent, but all found themselves facing charges of wilful sabotage, terrorism, and worse. Horror of horrors, however implausible the allegations, each vied with all the others to confess to the wildest imaginable crimes.

Now that we know what really happened, all these confessions read like nightmare fantasies. Not for nothing, during his own trial Bukharin himself described the confessions as 'a medieval principle of jurisprudence'. Gifted Western writers nevertheless embroidered these confessions, and the story of their victims, into highly compelling stories. *Darkness at Noon* by Arthur Koestler portrayed a thinly disguised Bukharin as the old Bolshevik Rubashov. Read today in the light of the knowledge we have, this sounds like raw, if clever, propaganda. Koestler thought Rubashov had confessed once it became clear that this was the last service he would be allowed to perform for the Party. But even in that charnel house there was no real masochist of such depravity as to offer such a service. Piety had its limits, and the trial victims were afforded ample scope to explore them. Kingsley Martin, the editor of the *New*

Statesman, described Koestler's as 'one of the few books written in this epoch which will survive it'.

The truth was altogether more simple. Bukharin had recently married a beautiful young bride, Anna Larina. She was half his age, and he was devoted to her. Their son, Yuri, was born during these events. It was unnecessary to torture Bukharin, because he would agree to anything possible to ensure the survival of his young wife and child. Stephen Cohen, Bukharin's biographer, has recorded what happened in some detail. The script which had been prepared for Bukharin by the managers of the trial was far-fetched in the extreme. This must have eased his efforts to cast doubt on the proceedings: but in the essential matter, he himself insisted on his own guilt, confessing to the most ludicrous charge of all, which affirmed his moral responsibility for all the many lesser wrongs which he specifically denied.

Later he was to write an extraordinary letter to Stalin, pleading for his life, in which he said:

'There is something great and bold about the political ideas of a general purge. It is

a) connected with the pre-war situation and
b) connected with the transition to democracy.
This purge encompasses
1) the guilty;
2) persons under suspicion; and 3) persons potentially under suspicion.
This business could not have been managed without me. Some are neutralized one way, others in another way, and a third group in yet another way. What serves as a guarantee for all this is the fact that people inescapably talk about each other and in doing so arouse an everlasting distrust in each other …

For God's sake, don't think that I am engaging here in reproaches, even in my inner thoughts. I wasn't born yesterday. I know all too well that *great* plans, *great* ideas, and *great* interests take precedence over everything, and I know that it would be petty for me to place the question of my own person on a par with the universal-historical tasks resting, first and foremost, on your shoulders …'

Before Bukharin was shot, Larina was already in deportation, and her child had been compulsorily adopted as an orphan.

In one of their last actual meetings, Bukharin gave Larina a letter, which he asked her to memorise. She took it into imprisonment in her head, and on her release from prison, but still in exile, she wrote it down several times, only to destroy it again for fear of discovery. Only in 1956, following the Twentieth Party Congress, did she keep a copy, which she later delivered to the Central Committee of the Communist Party, in 1961. This is the gist of what it said:

> 'I am leaving life. I am lowering my head not before the proletarian axe, which must be merciless but also virginal. I feel my helplessness before a hellish machine, which, probably by the use of medieval methods, has acquired gigantic power, fabricates organised slander, acts boldly and confidently ...
>
> Storm clouds have risen over the Party. My one head, guilty of nothing, will drag down thousands of guiltless heads. For an organisation must be created, a Bukharinite organisation, which is in reality not only non-existent now, the seventh year that I have had not a shadow of disagreement with the Party, but was also non-existent then, in the years of the right opposition. About the secret organisation of Riutin and Uglanov, I knew nothing. I expounded my views, together with Rykov and Tomskii, openly.
>
> I have been in the Party since I was eighteen, and the purpose of my life has always been to fight for the interests of the working class, for the victory of socialism ...
>
> I appeal to you, a future generation of Party

leaders, whose historical mission will include the obligation to take apart the monstrous cloud of crimes that is growing ever hungrier in these frightful times, taking fire like a flame and suffocating the Party.

I appeal to all Party members! In these days, perhaps the last of my life, I am confident that sooner or later the filter of history will inevitably sweep the filth from my head …

Know, comrades, that on that banner, which you will be carrying in the victorious march to communism, is also my drop of blood.'

N. Bukharin[2]

(The full text of his letter-testament is printed in chapter 2.)

Some of those who were closest to this tragedy found that they could only speak about it in parables. Perhaps the greatest such parable was composed by Bertolt Brecht, in one of his most famous plays. Brecht prepared a number of notes for this play, *The Life of Galileo*, even if he was unable to assemble them for publication. He prefaced them by saying:

'It is well known how felicitously people can be influenced by the conviction that they are poised on the threshold of a new age. At such a moment their environment appears to be still entirely unfinished, capable of the happiest improvements, full of dreamt of and undreamt of possibilities, like malleable raw material in their hands. They themselves feel as if they have awakened to a new day – rested, strong, resourceful. Old beliefs are dismissed as superstitions, what yesterday seemed a matter of course is today subject to fresh examination. We have been ruled, says mankind, but now we shall be the rulers.'

Bertolt Brecht, *The Life of Galileo*

How far Galileo thought like this may be disputed by scholars. But if Brecht was probably right about the new age of science in 1609, he was certainly right about the hoped for new age of politics in 1938.

Speaking less elliptically, he gave us his poem, *Is the People Infallible?* This was composed after Brecht's visit to the Soviet Union in Spring 1941, when he learnt of the death by shooting of his mentor, the writer Tretyakov. The same purge carried off his friend Karole Neger, and brought about the arrest of numerous German anti-fascists. Certainly, the poem is a memorial to Tretyakov. But it is also a critique, which laments the passing of so many other people, so many ideals.

1
My teacher
Tall and kindly
Has been shot, condemned by a people's court
As a spy. His name is damned.
His books are destroyed. Talk about him
Is suspect and suppressed.
Suppose he is innocent?

2
The sons of the people have found him guilty
The factories and collective farms
   of the workers
The world's most heroic institutions
Have identified him as an enemy.
No voice has been raised for him.
Suppose he is innocent?

3
The people has many enemies.
In the highest places
Sit enemies. In the most useful laboratories
Sit enemies. They build
Dykes and canals for the good
   of whole continents, and the canals
Silt up and the dykes
Collapse. The man in charge has to be shot.
Suppose he is innocent?

4
The enemy goes disguised.
He pulls a workman's cap over his eyes.
  His friends
Know him as a conscientious worker. His wife
Shows his leaky shoes
Worn out in the people's service.
And yet he is an enemy. Was my teacher
  one of them?
Suppose he is innocent?

5
To speak of the enemies that may be sitting in the
  people's courts
Is dangerous, for courts have reputations
  to keep up.
To ask for papers proving guilt
  in black and white
Is senseless, for there need be no such papers.
The criminals have proofs of their innocence to
  hand.
The innocent often have no proof.
Is it best to keep silent then?
Suppose he is innocent?

6
What 5000 have built one man can destroy.
Of 50 condemned

One may be guiltless.
Suppose he is innocent?

7
Suppose he is innocent
How will he go to his death?

* * *

Forty years on, the innocence of Bukharin had become abundantly plain. Khrushchev's Secret Speech to the Twentieth Congress of the Communist Party of the Soviet Union had made very clear that the wholesale repressions unleashed by Stalin in the thirties had involved multiple injustices, and the imprisonment and execution of very many people who were completely innocent.

Apparently Khrushchev had intended to re-examine the Moscow Trials, and rehabilitate some of their principal victims. But pressure from European Communist Parties, who had suffered mass defections when his original Secret Speech had been leaked out in 1956, prevented the continuation of Khrushchev's plans. Larina and her son began to petition the Soviet authorities for a reconsideration of the verdict on their famous relative. There were grounds for optimism. Speaking at the Twenty-second Congress in 1961, Khrushchev said:

> 'Perhaps we should erect a monument in Moscow to perpetuate the memory of the comrades who fell victim to arbitrary rule.'

But Khrushchev fell from power, and all talk of monuments went distinctly out of fashion.

From 1964 onwards there was little official room for objective recall of historical events, and we began to see the laborious growth of samizdat, the private circulation of manuscript copies of papers passed from hand to hand. One such document appeared soon after June 1977:

> 'Early in June 1977, an official of the Central Committee, Klimov, phoned at the apartment of A. M. Larina (N. I. Bukharin's widow) and asked that she get in touch with him. On June 9th, since A. M. Larina was out of Moscow, Yu. N. Larin, her son and son of N. I. Bukharin, called the number indicated by Klimov and asked him hadn't he phoned in connection with the letters sent by Bukharin's son and widow on the eve of the 25th Congress (of the Communist Party of the Soviet Union) to the Congress itself, to the Presidium of the Congress, to the Politburo of the Central Committee of the Communist Party of

the Soviet Union, and personally to the General Secretary of the CC, CPSU, L.I. Brezhnev, appealing for Bukharin's rehabilitation. Klimov confirmed that his call was connected with this matter and said the following:

> "I have been instructed to inform you that your appeal to have Bukharin reinstated in the Party and restored to full membership in the Academy of Sciences of the USSR cannot be granted since the guilty verdicts pertaining to the criminal offences for which he was tried have not been set aside".'

Yu. N. Larin replied that many of Bukharin's co-defendants have been rehabilitated; for example, Krestinsky, Ikramov, and Khodzhaev.

Klimov answered that obviously Larin didn't know that the majority of the accused at the trial had not been rehabilitated. Yu. N. Larin asked, 'Do you really believe that Nikolai Ivanovich (Bukharin) murdered Gorky?' Klimov answered: 'That question falls under the jurisdiction of the courts and the procurator's office.' Yu. N. Larin asked: 'Does that mean that you think I should turn to these bodies?' To this Klimov answered: 'That's your right,' but made it clear he ought not do that at the present time. 'You should know how complicated the situation is now.'

A. M. Larina and Yu. N. Larin first appealed for N. I. Bukharin's rehabilitation in 1961. Thus

> the rejection came 16 years after the first request and a year and a half after the last. (V. I. Lenin's friends, E. D. Stasova and V. A. Karpinsky, having made an analogous appeal in 1965, died and consequently never got an answer.)
>
> Having received the foregoing statement, Yu. N. Larin addressed a petition for Bukharin's rehabilitation to the Chairman of the Supreme Court of the USSR on June 11th, 1977.'[3]

It having become clear that further petitions to Soviet officialdom would not avail, Larin decided to send his appeal further afield. That is why he wrote to the Italian Communist leader, Enrico Berlinguer, who had an international reputation for greater open-mindedness than was customary among an earlier generation of European Communist leaders.

'Respected Comrade Berlinguer,
> I am writing this letter to you on the eve of the 40th anniversary of the tragic death of my father, Nikolai Ivanovich Bukharin. At that time I was only two years old and naturally was unable to remember my father. But my mother, who had spent many years in Stalin's prisons and camps, miraculously survived and told me the truth about my father. Later G. M. Krzhizhanovsky, one of V. I. Lenin's

closest friends, and Old Bolsheviks, who had lived through the terror and who had known Nikolai Ivanovich in one circumstance or another, told me about him. In addition I read many Bolshevik books (which are banned in our country even today and have been preserved only by chance by certain Old Bolsheviks) including books by Nikolai Ivanovich himself and the works of foreign researchers. The information which I obtained in this way helped me to fully appreciate the character and the social and political activity of my father. I understood the enormity of Stalin's crimes, the extent to which he had falsified the history of the Party, the absurdity and stupidity of the accusations levelled against my father at the Plenum of the Central Committee of February/March 1937 and the trial of the so-called "Right-Trotskyist Bloc". However, on the basis of these absurd charges (espionage, treason, sabotage and murder), my father was expelled from the Central Committee and from the Party and condemned to death.

Beginning in 1961 my mother A. M. Larin and then I myself persistently raised with the highest Party-State organs of the country the question of the withdrawal of the monstrous allegations against N. I. Bukharin and his restoration to Party membership. This question was also raised with the Party leadership by the most senior of the Old Bolsheviks led by the former secretary of the Central Committee of the Party, E. D. Stasova. They died some time ago without receiving an answer and it was only last summer (1977) that we at last received some response in the form of a telephone call. An official of the Commission of Party Control of the Central Committee of the CPSU informed us by telephone that the accusations made at the trial of Bukharin had not been withdrawn as the process of examining the documents relating to the trial had not been completed; the question of the restoration of his Party membership could not, therefore, yet be resolved. This means that 40 years after the execution of my father we have received an answer, which, in effect, confirms the monstrous charges of Stalin. My approach to the Courts (the Supreme Court of the USSR) has been fruitless: the simple truth is they don't answer me.

In a country where the greater part of the

population has been brought up on the mendacious *Short Course [History of the Communist Party of the Soviet Union (Bolsheviks)]* there are many who still consider my father as a traitor and a hireling-of-Hitler although in reality the truth is that he was an outstanding fighter against fascism and in his last years he devoted all his energies to the exposure of fascism and to warnings against the growing fascist threat.

Leaving home for the last time for the Plenum of February/March 1937 (from which he never returned) my father said to my mother "don't become embittered: there are sad errors in history. I want my son to grow up as a Bolshevik". He looked on the events which had occurred as tragic but transient; he believed in the ultimate victory of the forces of socialism.

I am not a member of the Party but for my father the word "Bolshevik" undoubtedly means a fighter for social justice. And we are unable to obtain such justice in our country for a man whom Lenin before his death called "the favourite of the whole Party". For my mother, who lived through the horrors of Stalin's camps, who knew many of Lenin's comrades-in-arms, representatives of the old Bolshevik Party – people about whom she preserves in her memory the happiest recollections and of whom she always speaks with tenderness and love – life in such a situation is becoming more and more intolerable. It is inconceivable that people who still carry on their shoulders the burden of Stalin's crimes and have not cast it into the dustbin of history can fight for high ideals.

I am approaching you, Comrade Berlinguer, not only because you are the leader of the largest communist party of western Europe and have thrown off this burden but also because N. I. Bukharin was a Communist-Internationalist, an active member of the International Workers' Movement. He was known to Communists of many countries: they always recalled him with warmth. Some of them are still living and are working in the ranks of the Italian Communist Party. I particularly have in mind Comrade Umberto Terracini.

I am approaching you to ask you to participate in the campaign for the rehabilitation of my father, in whatever form seems to you to be most appropriate.

Not long before his death Nikolai

Ivanovich wrote a letter "to the future generation of leaders of the Party" in which he appealed to them "to unravel the monstrous tangle of crimes". My mother learnt the text of this letter by heart in the dark days and after her rehabilitation she passed it on to the Central Committee of the Party. This letter ended with the words:

> "Know Comrades that on the banner which you will carry in your victorious march towards communism there is a drop of my blood."
>
> Yours sincerely,
> Yu. Larin (Bukharin) 12.3.78'

But Berlinguer did not reply, and it was at this point that I received a copy of Larin's letter at the Russell Foundation, and we decided to circulate it, in order to encourage a response. Numerous Socialist and Communist leaders signed our appeal to the Soviet Government to reopen the Bukharin case. But from Italy, a group of distinguished Socialist leaders, led by Riccardo Lombardi, soon persuaded a number of Communist intellectuals to join in. Some legendary names from the earliest days of Italian Communism, old enough to have been friends of Bukharin, spoke up. So it came about that Enrico Berlinguer encouraged the Istituto Gramsci to convene a symposium on the work of Bukharin, inviting a wide range of Sovietologists and other relevant scholars to participate.

The symposium was held, in 1980, at a beautiful summer school in Frattocchie, placed in a flower garden, and as far removed as is imaginable from cells of the Lubyanka. Bukharin's biographer, Stephen Cohen, had only recently published his book, which was receiving critical plaudits. He was a star participant in the seminar. Numerous other scholars also joined in. They included Alec Nove, Guiseppe Boffa, Adolf Lowy, Giuliano Procacci, Aldo Zanardo, Moshe Lewin, Robert C. Tucker, Wlodzimierz Brus, Alexander Erlich and, of course, Paolo Spriano.

Part of this galaxy of talent was a shy Chinese scholar, Su Shaozhi, who was at the time Deputy Director of the Institute of Marxism, Leninism, Mao Tse-Tung Thought. He was curious about Bukharin, but had not had access to any of his writings, and knew very little about his troubled history. We began talking, and when the seminar adjourned, we continued our discussion through the night. Indeed, we had more than one late night session, as Su pumped me for every crumb of information I could give him about the Bukharin case. He took a copy of my booklet on this, and subsequently arranged for it to be translated into Chinese. It was published in 70,000 copies soon afterwards, and we began a protracted correspondence which covered numerous other issues. I must have sent dozens of books to China on a wide variety of topics. Many of them were widely circulated through Su's Institute.

Subsequently I made many visits to China on behalf of the burgeoning European peace movement, European Nuclear Disarmament. I found myself surrounded by Chinese students who were keen to press questions on me. One of them said it all: 'Is alienation possible in a Socialist society?' Before the demonstration at Tiananmen Square, such heavy matters preoccupied an influential part of the Chinese youth movement.

But the interest in Bukharin did not restrict itself to historical and philosophical questions. Evidently, China was going through an intensive debate on the relationship between socialism and democracy and the works of Bukharin were being combed for insights on economic policy. From this distance, and without helpful translators, I find it difficult to follow the development of these arguments in the twenty-first century. But there is no doubt that they are continuing, and have a momentum of their own.

In 1991, James D. White contributed a paper to *Soviet Studies*, entitled 'Chinese Studies of Bukharin'.[4] This reported that following an eclipse of Chinese interest from the time of the trial until the end of the 1970s, a fresh interest began to be shown in Bukharin's works. I think it is possible that my pamphlet inaugurated this phase in Bukharin studies.

James D. White interests himself in the development of the commodity economy, and the connection between Bukharin's economic thought and official Chinese doctrine on the part played by markets in the development of the overall economy. As White points out, in the USSR the rehabilitation of Bukharin was part of a process which opened up debate on the existing political structure, and undermined the official history which had buttressed those arrangements. But in China, Bukharin could become an inspiration for 'the Chinese economic reforms and the transition to a more market-oriented form of socialism'.

The collapse of the Soviet Union collapsed a

significant part of the interest in Soviet history, and encouraged more flippant approaches to it. Far from diminishing, propaganda responses were augmented, in a world in which the evil empire had imploded. But Bukharin's ghost does still apparently walk in China, whether or not it facilitates good works in the long run.

In Russia, the archaeological work of Stephen Cohen excavated a mass of Bukharin legacies. The books upon which he worked in prison have all been published. They are of variable quality. It was not easy to carry on sustained intellectual work under prison conditions, although Bukharin had a phenomenal mind, and there is much of interest in what he left behind, however lugubrious the circumstances under which he toiled.

But another legacy, more traumatic than any of these books, is to be found in Bukharin's letter to Stalin on the 10th December 1937. We append this below.

In appealing for his life, Bukharin proposes that he be exiled to America in order to wage a final campaign against Trotsky's ideas and win over the wavering intelligentsia. The lack of realism in this proposal, quite apart from its outrageous morality, reflects the miasma in which Bukharin had been living before and after his imprisonment. As Cohen himself reports, Bukharin had been exposed to unbelievable stresses under unbearable moral pressure. But further, Stalin had absolutely no need for help in dealing with the problem of Trotsky. His plans for this were well advanced, and had nothing to do with refuting undesirable opinion. Thought stops when life is extinguished, and the KGB was actively preparing for the assasination, which, it was believed, would put a stop to this troublesome heretic. Tragic though the death of Bukharin was to be, it had nothing of the grandeur of the life of Trotsky, who was able to defy the tyranny to the bitter end, and went to his grave an integral personality, uncompromised and complete.

References

1. *Shipwreck of a Generation*, Harvill, 1971, pp. 99-100. This book contains a graphic description of Bukharin's intervention at the 1934 Writers' Congress, the details of which are currently the subject of dispute among independent scholars.
2. This letter is reproduced from Roy Medvedev's *Let History Judge*, pp. 183-4. If there is one indispensable book on the whole background to this case, this is it. Amongst other things, it points out some of the errors in Bukharin's own assumptions in this moving document.
3. This document was published in the American Socialist newspaper, *In These Times*, November 16-22, 1977, p.13.
4. J. D. White: *Soviet Studies*, volume 43, no. 4, 1991, pp. 733-747.

Bukharin and Trotsky shown as a two-headed monster labelled 'The Right-Trotskyist Monstrosity'. The hand holding them back bears the label 'Gestapo'.

2
Bukharin's testament

TO A FUTURE GENERATION OF PARTY LEADERS

'I am leaving life. I am lowering my head not before the proletarian axe, which must be merciless but also virginal. I feel my helplessness before a hellish machine, which, probably by the use of medieval methods, has acquired gigantic power, fabricates organised slander, acts boldly and confidently.

Dzerzhinskii is gone; the remarkable traditions of the Cheka have gradually faded into the past, when the revolutionary idea guided all its actions, justified cruelty to enemies, guarded the state against any kind of counter-revolution. That is how the Cheka earned special confidence, special respect, authority and esteem. At present, most of the so-called organs of the NKVD are a degenerate organisation of bureaucrats, without ideas, rotten, well-paid, who use the Cheka's bygone authority to cater to Stalin's morbid suspiciousness (I fear to say more) in a scramble for rank and fame, concocting their slimy cases, not realising that they are at the same time destroying themselves – history does not put up with witnesses of foul deeds.

Any member of the Central Committee, any member of the Party can be rubbed out, turned into a traitor, terrorist, diversionist, spy, by these "wonder-working organs". If Stalin should ever get any doubts about himself, confirmation would instantly follow.

Storm clouds have risen over the Party. My one head, guilty of nothing, will drag down thousands of guiltless heads. For an organisation must be created, a Bukharinite organisation, which is in reality not only non-existent now, the seventh year that I have had not a shadow of disagreement with the Party, but was also non-existent then, in the years of the right opposition. About the secret organisation of Riutin and Uglanov, I knew nothing. I expounded my views, together with Rykov and Tomskii, openly.

I have been in the Party since I was eighteen, and the purpose of my life has always been to fight for the interests of the working class, for the victory of socialism. These days the paper with the sacred name *Pravda* prints the filthiest lie, that I, Nikolai Bukharin, have wished to destroy the triumphs of October, to restore capitalism. That is unexampled insolence, that is a lie that could be equalled in insolence, in irresponsibility to the people, only by such a lie as this: it has been discovered that Nikolai Romanov devoted his whole life to the struggle against capitalism and monarchy, to the struggle for the achievement of a proletarian revolution. If, more than once, I was mistaken about the methods of building socialism, let posterity judge me no more harshly than Vladimir Illich did. We were moving towards a single goal for the first time, on a still unblazed trail. Other times, other customs. *Pravda* carried a discussion page, everyone argued, searched for ways and means, quarrelled and made up and moved on together.

I appeal to you, a future generation of Party leaders, whose historical mission will include the obligation to take apart the monstrous cloud of crimes that is growing ever hungrier in these frightful times, taking fire like a flame and suffocating the Party.

I appeal to all Party members! In these days, perhaps the last of my life, I am confident that sooner or later the filter of history will inevitably sweep the filth from my head. I was never a traitor; without hesitation I would have given my life for Lenin's. I loved Kirov, started nothing against Stalin. I ask a new young and honest generation of Party leaders to read my letter at a Party Plenum, to exonerate me, and to reinstate me in the Party.

Know, comrades, that on that banner, which you will be carrying in the victorious march to communism, is also my drop of blood.'

N. Bukharin

Bukharin's wife, Anna Larina, who memorised his testament.

3
Bukharin's letter to Stalin

'VERY SECRET [ves'ma sekretno]
PERSONAL
Request no one be allowed to read this letter without the express permission of I. V. Stalin.

To: I.V. Stalin. 7 pages + 7 pages of memoranda.

Iosif Vissarionovich:

This is perhaps the last letter I shall write to you before my death. That's why, though I am a prisoner, I ask you to permit me to write this letter without resorting to officialese [ofitsial'shchina], all the more so since I am writing this letter to you alone: the very fact of its existence or non-existence will remain entirely in your hands.

I've come to the last page of my drama and perhaps of my very life. I agonized over whether I should pick up pen and paper – as I write this, I am shuddering all over from disquiet and from a thousand emotions stirring within me, and I can hardly control myself. But precisely because I have so little time left, I want to take my leave of you in advance, before it's too late, before my hand ceases to write, before my eyes close, while my brain somehow still functions.

In order to avoid any misunderstandings, I will say to you from the outset that, as far as the world at large (society) is concerned:

a) I have no intention of recanting anything I've written down [confessed];
b) In this sense (or in connection with this), I have no intention of asking you or of pleading with you for anything that might derail my case from the direction in which it is heading. But I am writing to you for your personal information. I cannot leave this life without writing to you these last lines because I am in the grip of torments which you should know about.
1) Standing on the edge of a precipice, from which there is no return, I tell you on my word of honour, as I await my death, that I am innocent of those crimes which I admitted to at the investigation.
2) Reviewing everything in my mind – insofar as I can – I can only add the following observations to what I have already said at the plenum:

a) I once heard someone say that someone had yelled out something. It seems to me that it was Kuzmin, but I had never ascribed any real significance to it – it had never even entered my mind;

b) Aikhenvald told me in passing, post factum, as we walked on the street, about the conference which I knew nothing about (nor did I know anything about the Riutin Platform) ("the gang has met, and a report was read") – or something of the sort. And, yes, I concealed this fact, feeling pity for the "gang".

c) I was also guilty of engaging in duplicity in 1932 in my relations with my "followers", believing sincerely that I would thereby win them back wholly to the Party. Otherwise, I'd have alienated them from the Party. That was all there was to it. In saying this, I am clearing my conscience totally. All the rest either never took place or, if it did, then I had no inkling of it whatsoever.

So at the plenum I spoke the truth and nothing but the truth, but no one believed me. And here and now I speak the absolute truth: all these past years, I have been honestly and sincerely carrying out

the Party line and have learned to cherish and love you wisely.
3) I had no "way out" other than that of confirming the accusations and testimonies of others and of elaborating on them. Otherwise, it would have turned out that I had not "disarmed".
4) Apart from extraneous factors and apart from argument #3 above, I have formed, more or less, the following conception of what is going on in our country:

There is something great and bold about the political ideas of a general purge. It is a) connected with the pre-war situation and b) connected with the transition to democracy. This purge encompasses 1) the guilty; 2) persons under suspicion; and 3) persons potentially under suspicion. This business could not have been managed without me. Some are neutralized one way, others in another way, and a third group in yet another way. What serves as a guarantee for all this is the fact that people inescapably talk about each other and in doing so arouse an everlasting distrust in each other. (I'm judging from my own experience. How I raged against Radek, who had smeared me, and then I myself following in his wake ...)

In this way, the leadership is bringing about a full guarantee for itself.

For God's sake, don't think that I am engaging here in reproaches, even in my inner thoughts. I wasn't born yesterday. I know all too well that great plans, great ideas, and great interests take precedence over everything, and I know that it would be petty for me to place the question of my own person on a par with the universal-historical tasks resting, first and foremost, on your shoulders. But it is here that I feel my deepest agony and find myself facing my chief, agonizing paradox.

5) If I were absolutely sure that your thoughts ran precisely along this path, then I would feel so much more at peace with myself. Well, so what! If it must be so, then so be it! But believe me, my heart boils over when I think that you might believe that I am guilty of these crimes and that in your heart of hearts you yourself think that I am really guilty of all of these horrors. In that case, what would it mean? Would it turn out that I have been helping to deprive [the Party] of many people (beginning with myself!) – that is, that I am wittingly committing an evil?! In that case, such action could never be justified. My

head is giddy with confusion, and I feel like yelling at the top of my voice. I feel like pounding my head against the wall: for, in that case, I have become a cause for the death of others. What am I to do? What am I to do?

6) I bear not one iota of malice toward anyone, nor am I bitter. I am not a Christian. But I do have my quirks. I believe that I am suffering retribution for those years when I really waged a campaign. And if you really want to know, more than anything else I am oppressed by one fact, which you have perhaps forgotten: once, most likely during the summer of 1928, I was at your place, and you said to me: "Do you know why I consider you my friend? After all, you are not capable of intrigues, are you?" And I said: "No I am not." At that time, I was hanging around with Kamenev ("first encounter"). Believe it or not, but it is this fact that stands out in my mind as original sin does for a Jew [sic]. Oh, God, what a child I was! What a fool! And now I'm paying for this with my honour and with my life. For this forgive me, Koba. I weep as I write. I no longer need anything, and you yourself know that I am probably making my

situation worse by allowing myself to write all this. But I just can't, I simply can't keep silent, I must give you my final "farewell". It is for this reason that I bear no malice towards anyone, not towards the [Party-state] leadership nor the investigators nor anyone in between. I ask you for forgiveness, though I have already been punished to such an extent that everything has grown dim around me, and darkness has descended upon me.

7) When I was hallucinating, I saw you several times and once I saw Nadezhda Sergeevna [Stalin's second wife who died in 1932]. She approached me and said: "What have they done with you, Nikolai Ivanovich? I'll tell Iosif to bail you out." This was so real that I was about to jump and write a letter to you and ask you to … bail me out! Reality had become totally mixed up in my mind with delusion. I know that Nadezhda Sergeevna would never believe that I had harboured any evil thoughts against you, and not for nothing did the subconscious of my wretched self cause this delusion in me. We talked for hours, you and I … Oh, Lord, if only there were some device which would have made it possible for you to see my soul

flayed and ripped open! If only you could see how I am attached to you, body and soul, quite unlike certain people such as Stetsky or Tal. Well, so much for "psychology" – forgive me. No angel will appear now to snatch Abraham's sword from his hand. My fatal destiny shall be fulfilled.

8) Permit me, finally, to move on to my last, minor, requests.

   a) It would be a thousand times easier for me to die than to go through the coming trial: I simply don't know how I'll be able to control myself – you know my nature: I am not an enemy either of the Party or of the USSR, and I'll do all within my powers [to serve the Party's cause], but, under such circumstances, my powers are minimal, and heavy emotions rise up in my soul. I'd get on my knees, forgetting shame and pride, and plead with you not to make me go through with it [the trial]. But this is probably already impossible. I'd ask you, if it were possible, to let me die before the trial. Of course, I know how harshly you look upon such matters.

   b) If I'm to receive the death sentence, then I implore you beforehand, I entreat you, by all that you hold dear, not to have me shot. Let me drink poison in my cell instead. (Let me have morphine so that I can fall asleep and never wake up.) For me, this point is extremely important. I don't know what words I should summon up in order to entreat you to grant me this as an act of charity. After all, politically, it won't really matter, and, besides, no one will know a thing about it. But let me spend my last moments as I wish. Have pity on me! Surely you'll understand – knowing me as well as you do. Sometimes I look death openly in the face, just as I know very well that I am capable of brave deeds. At other times, I, ever the same person, find myself in such disarray that I am drained of all strength. So if the verdict is death, let me have a cup of morphine. I implore you …

c) I ask you to allow me to bid farewell to my wife and son. No need for me to say goodbye to my daughter. I feel sorry for her. It will be too painful for her. It will also be too painful to Nadya and my father. Anyuta, on the other hand, is young. She will survive. I would like to exchange a few last words with her. I would like permission to meet her before the trial. My argument is as follows: if my family sees what I confessed to, they might commit suicide from sheer unexpectedness. I must somehow prepare them for it. It seems to me that this is in the interests of the case and its official interpretation.

d) If, contrary to expectation, my life is to be spared, I would like to request (though I would first have to discuss it with my wife) the following:

i) That I be exiled to America for x numbers of years. My arguments are: I would myself wage a campaign [in favour] of the trials, I would wage a mortal war against Trotsky, I would win over large segments of the wavering intelligentsia, I would in effect become Anti-Trotsky and would carry out this mission in a big way and, indeed, with much zeal. You could send an expert security officer [chekist] with me and, as added insurance, you could detain my wife here for six months until I have proven that I am really punching Trotsky and Company in the nose, etc.

ii) But if there is the slightest doubt in your mind, then exile me to a camp in Pechora or Kolyma, even for 25 years. I could set up there the following: a university, a museum of local culture, technical stations, and so on, institutes, a painting gallery, an ethnographic museum, a zoological and botanical museum, a camp newspaper and journal.

In short, settling there with my family to the end of my days, I would carry out pioneering, enterprising, cultural work.

In any case, I declare that I would work like a dynamo wherever I am sent.

However, to tell the truth, I do not place much hope in this since the very fact of a change in the directive of the February plenum speaks for itself (and I see all too well that things point to a trial taking place any day now).

And so these, it seems, are my last requests (one more thing: my philosophical work, remaining after me – I have done a lot of useful work in it).

Iosif Vissarionovich! In me you have lost one of your most capable generals, one who is genuinely devoted to you. But that is all past. I remember that Marx wrote that Alexander the First lost a great helper to no purpose in Barclay de Tolly after the latter was charged with treason. It is bitter to reflect on all this. But I am preparing myself mentally to depart from this vale of tears, and there is nothing in me towards all of you, towards the Party and the cause, but a great and boundless love. I am doing everything that is humanly possible and impossible. I have written to you about all this. I have crossed all the t's and dotted all the i's. I have done all this in advance, since I have no idea at all what condition I shall be in tomorrow and the day after tomorrow, etc. Being a neurasthenic, I shall perhaps feel such universal apathy that I won't be able even so much as to move my finger.

But now in spite of a headache and with tears in my eyes, I am writing. My conscience is clear before you now, Koba. I ask you one final time for your forgiveness (only in your heart, not otherwise). For that reason I embrace you in my mind. Farewell forever and remember kindly your wretched

        N. Bukharin 10th December 1937'

4
'I was a Bukharin'
Interview with Yuri Larin, the son of Nikolai Bukharin.

This interview was first published in July 2008 in the journal of the Russkiy Mir Foundation. It is reprinted with grateful acknowledgements.

The year 2008 marked the 120th anniversary of the birth and the 70th anniversary of the death of Nikolai Bukharin. Stalin once told him: 'You and I, Bukharchik, are the Himalayas. The others are little blots.' However, Stalin later did everything not only to destroy Bukharin, but also to erase all memory of him. Bukharin's son, Yuri, having spent the first few months of his life in the Kremlin, wound up spending many years in an orphanage with no idea who his real parents were. Today, Yuri Larin is a renowned artist. His water-colours hang in Russia's largest museums and can be found in private collections around the world.

You were slightly older than two when your father was executed and your mother was arrested. Life deprived you not only of your father's last name, but also a patronymic. How were you able to get it back?

It so happened that my last name changed on several occasions. When I was born, I was a Bukharin. When my parents were arrested, I was taken in by my relatives, by the family of Boris Gusman. Thus, several decades ago, instead of becoming Yuri Nikolayevich Bukharin, I became Yuri Borisovich Gusman. Then the Gusmans were arrested as well and I ended up in an orphanage. When an opportunity finally arose for me to change my last name, there was a law that prohibited the patronymic from being changed. For this reason, I remained Borisovich until *Perestroika* when Bukharin was completely rehabilitated.

My present last name, Larin, is my mother's, whom I met again when I turned nineteen. I came to see her in her settlement in Siberia. My mother got that last name not from her parents but from her adopted family, which took her up as a one-year old baby after her real mother died. Larin was a well-known revolutionary and his wife was my mother's aunt. For the longest time, Larin was a member of the State Planning Committee, and the head of the economic department of the All-Russian Central Executive Committee. Since he was physically disabled from birth, in order to make his work easier for him, many of the meetings were conducted directly in his office. That was when my mother, still a little girl, first met her future husband, Nikolai Bukharin.

Were you ever told your family history?

No, I never knew a thing, and for the longest time I believed that the Gusmans were my real parents. Even when I came to see my mother for the first time in 1956, even then I could only guess as to who my real father was. I asked my mother about this on the very first day, and she said that my father was a well-known Bolshevik who was convicted during the trials of the 1930s. Since my mother told me about my grandfather, Ivan Gavrilovich, I tried to guess which of the convicted party members was an Ivanovich. And I told mother that it was probably Bukharin, since he was a Nikolai Ivanovich and was accused of organizing the right wing. My mother never expected me to guess correctly so quickly.

Bukharin was recognized as an outstanding economist, but also a pretty good artist. The renowned artist Konstantin Yuon once told him: 'Forget about politics. There is no future in politics for you. Painting is your real calling.' When did you start painting yourself?

I can't say for sure when exactly it happened, or whether it can even be called painting. Perhaps it was when I designed wall newspapers at the orphanage. After I left there, I studied at the Novocherkassk Engineering and Land Reclamation Institute, and I only arrived in Moscow in the early 1960s. The first museum I ever visited was the Pushkin Museum. The first painter that I fell in love with was Albert Marquet. Everything in his works amazed me. For example, he painted a bridge over the Seine, with some people walking across. I looked at it and thought: 'How interesting – you cannot take the image of a single person out of this painting without ruining the wholeness if its composition.' I did not understand a single thing about art at the time, but I already sensed talent when I saw it.

After returning to Moscow, I enrolled in a correspondence course at the Krupskaya Arts University. That was when I met my future wife, Inga, who was studying to become an architect and who taught me a lot about art. By the way, it was her box of paints that first prompted me to try my hand at painting. I started painting small landscapes, and the institute instructors gave me feedback on each of my works.

By that time, I had already spent several years working as a planner. I would travel the country on assignments and they even sent me to Romania, which was not bad at all for a young man in those days. It seemed that my life was already determined for me many years in advance. And then suddenly, while standing in a cafeteria line, one of my co-workers told me that he had read an announcement about the Stroganov Academy enrolling students for their design department. They were looking for people who had already received an education in either engineering or the arts.

I managed to get accepted and I remain very grateful to that academy because I had some amazing teachers. For example, there was Ivan Lamtsov, who taught us a discipline that was banned in the 1930s – architectonics or architectural composition. Today, it even seems bizarre why this subject needed to be banned. I feel like I was simply lucky that fate brought me to the Stroganov Academy. It allowed me to be a designer by profession, but I knew from the very start that I would actually be painting.

Many children of famous parents live like parasites off their families' histories. But you, on the other hand, never tried to use Bukharin's name to draw attention to yourself as an artist.

People have different views of my father. Perhaps those who use their parents' fame never had this ambiguity and these difficulties. After all, Bukharin was rehabilitated not even after the famous 20th Congress, when Stalin's crimes were first denounced, but much later than that, during *Perestroika* – despite the fact that my mother and I had filed repeated appeals for his case to be reviewed. But today, as far as I know, Bukharin's views are studied in economic history courses.

On the other hand, I feel that we are still waiting for an interpretation of who Bukharin truly was. For example, I was watching a documentary recently, and it seemed that his name should have been mentioned, but it never came up even once. Lenin himself called Nikolai Bukharin 'a favourite of the entire party'. The people liked him very much as well. In her memoirs, my mother recalls how in the Altai taiga, a local hunter came to Bukharin and brought him some flat cakes that were baked by his wife, and all because he considered Bukharin to be a defender of the peasantry. During *Perestroika*, many economists wrote that if Bukharin's course of developing agriculture had been selected instead of Stalin's forced collectivization, Russia would have been able to avoid both famine and repression of the peasantry, and that it would have taken much less time to feed the country.

Stalin never was able to forgive Bukharin for his phrase about politics 'causing a quarrel between the country and the peasant'. How long did the process of repressing Bukharin last?

Bukharin was arrested immediately after his trip to Pamir. He was returning to Moscow aware that Zinoviev, Kamenev, Sokolnikov and Radek had by then denounced both him and themselves by signing confessions about those phantasmagoric spy cells. Today, we know how such confessions were obtained. Bukharin could not avoid such a fate either.

He spent two years in jail before his execution. He continued to write in jail, finding writing to be his only solace. The early 1990s saw the publication of the *Philosophical*

Arabesques, which he wrote at the time, as well as his novel about childhood called *How it All Began*. But he also left behind more than 120 prison poems. For the longest time, they were stored in the presidential archive. Recently, I sent them to the Academy of Sciences' archive, because to be honest, I didn't know whether they should be published, or whether they were even good enough.

But you like them?

I wouldn't say that. But then, I don't really consider myself to be a connoisseur of poetry. Bukharin wrote the poems at night, often after his interrogations, and of course they reflect his psychological state at the time. Many of them are now viewed as his effort to engage in psychotherapy. However, it seems to me that in certain poems, you can detect a coded message and a certain 'cosmism', one that shares something with the works of Zabolotsky and the ideas of Vernadsky. Some 340 pages of poetry remain. In some of them, you can even find the world of grass, in others, the world of human relations. Some also contain philosophical musings.

Bukharin never wrote poetry before he was

in jail, but he knew poetry very well. It was no accident that one of his best speeches is considered to be the report he made about poetry at the writers' congress. He was even recognised by those he criticized in his report. As far as Zabolotsky is concerned, Bukharin was in awe of his poetry, and they were friends for many years.

By the way, *Pravda* once published an enormous article attacking Zabolotsky. So Bukharin, who was the editor-in-chief of *Izvestia* at the time, asked Zabolotsky to send him a few of his poems, and then he published them. The poems were terrific, but after that *Pravda* article, not many would have dared to take such a step. Later, Zabolotsky himself was accused of standing in favour of Bukharin's positions, and this made his life complicated for a long time.

But if we go back to Bukharin's poetry, I can say that I received a letter from the academician Wyacheslav Ivanov in which he mentioned an upcoming meeting of the Pasternak Commission. They are going to review publications on the subject of 'Pasternak and Bukharin'. And they might even discuss the publication of Bukharin's poems.

Your mother, Anna Larina, spoke in her memoirs

about how she also began writing poetry while in prison. Apparently, they helped her survive. Whose ideas was it to write a book of memoirs?

Probably mine. I bought mother a notebook and told her that she had better not go a day without writing a line. But it was never meant to prove anything to anyone – it was solely for herself. She spent 19 years in various prisons, camps and exile. After the death of her second husband, whom she met while in exile, she was left with two children on her hands, and I was sick with a severe form of tuberculosis at the time. So things were far from easy for her after her rehabilitation. It seemed to me that only by writing a book of memoirs would she be able to begin a new stage in life, to free herself of the injustices of the past.

When Bukharin was arrested, one of his last words to your mother was: 'Please, do not become embittered!' Judging by her book, Anna Larina, a phenomenal beauty who inspired awe in everyone, could never turn bitter, even after all her incredible ordeals. What about you? Do you ever feel bitter about your fate?

No, I don't. Many had as hard a time as my family did at the time. I am grateful to my relatives, who took me, a one-year-old, out of the orphanage. Boris Gusman was a tremendous construction engineer, and once even participated in the construction of Lenin's Mausoleum. After the evacuation, his family moved to Stalingrad, but he was arrested almost immediately after the war. I wound up in a Stalingrad children's home that I only have fond memories of. We had wonderful teachers. People say lots of bad things about children's homes, but no one ever bullied me. And by the way, to this day, I am still friends with the son of our director.

I think that fate, which had so many ordeals in store for our family, not only brought us bad, but also some good surprises. There's one story I can tell you, for example. When my wife and I had our son, we named him Nikolai in honour of Bukharin. We had nowhere to live. Our acquaintance, Alexei Snegov, who spent 18 years in the camps, advised me to turn to Mikoyan for help. At first I thought that trying to turn directly to Mikoyan was completely useless – especially since in 1937, Mikoyan had headed the commission assigned to find Bukharin guilty. However, several weeks after my conversation with Mikoyan, I was handed the keys to a two-room apartment. This was already in the Brezhnev era.

Artists without a famous last name had a hard time surviving in the Soviet Union. How did you reconcile the dilemma of surviving while continuing to create?

When I received my degree in design, I asked my teacher: 'What do I do next?' And he replied that in his opinion, the best thing to do was to teach, since you have a lot of free time left over for painting. So that is what I did. For 15 years, I worked as a teacher at the Memory of 1905 Art School. I taught for three days a week, and on the fourth, I painted.

Was it difficult for you to find a common language with your students?

At first, it was very difficult. Especially with the first group, which noticed that I knew little at the time. I was recently at an arts exhibition where I met a student from that first group – Ksenya Shimanovkaya. She is now a famous stage designer. So I asked her if they had noticed my lack of professionalism at the time. And I was very surprised that she praised my lessons after all these years. Maybe I was helped by the fact that back at the Stroganov Academy, I took photographs of some terrific paintings. I would then show these pictures to my students and used them as an example to analyze various cases and ways in which the compositions were constructed.

When did you become known specifically as a painter?

Recognition probably only came to me in 1982. Before then, I participated in several exhibitions, but only that year's exhibition really brought me any attention. It was held in the foyer of the Yermolov Theatre, and my works made it there thanks to my friend, the painter Valery Volkov. His exhibition was a great success and made my name famous.

After my big exhibition in 1989, the Russian Museum purchased tens of my water-colours, and one water-colour was acquired by the Tretyakov Gallery. The paintings also went to various museums across the country. However, I consider one of my greatest successes to be the Radishchev Museum in Saratov expressing interest in my paintings and acquiring several of them for its exhibition. This also happened pretty much by accident. One of this museum's former staff members moved to suburban Moscow. She was told about my exhibition, which was being staged at the Bulgarian

Cultural Centre at the time. She dropped by and she liked it so much that this woman immediately called Saratov, saying that they must definitely stage a Larin exhibition. They sent a museum truck over to my place, took away my works, staged a wonderful exhibition and even purchased a few paintings for the museum.

Your works were highly valued by Italy's former ambassador to Russia. How did you get to know him?

Back in his time, Bukharin surrounded himself with lots of talented students. People once spoke about the 'Bukharin school of economics', but after the Stalin trials, it was pejoratively called 'the little school'. Well, Nikolai Ivanovich's students included Alexander Aikhenvald. His father was once exiled on the famous Philosophy steamer, while Alexander himself was a convinced communist. But a sincere belief in communism did not save him from execution. He left behind a son, Yuri Aikhenvald, who went through exile and the insane asylum. He was someone I became friends with. He decided to show my works to the renowned Moscow collector Rubenstein. When Rubenstein came to our place, he noticed a still-unfinished work, a portrait of my son Kolya dressed in a carnival costume, and he said: 'A splendid portrait'. I replied that I had only begun working on it. 'Begun?' Rubenstein asked. 'It looks completely finished to me'. So I decided to leave it as it was. Rubenstein purchased six of my works, and it was a great pleasure for me to see that he hung these paintings at home, next to those of Larionov and other famous artists.

Rubenstein was an incredibly sociable person and once introduced me to the wife of the Italian ambassador, who was walking her dog. Rubenstein began introducing the ambassador's wife to the works of Moscow artists and once invited her to my exhibition. She came with her husband, the Italian ambassador, who asked whether he could visit me at home. He then purchased a few of my works. I feel like this story was a chain of lucky coincidences from the very start.

I have generally been lucky to meet good people. When they took away my arts studio because the property prices in the centre of Moscow were so high that lots of contenders wanted the space, the surgeon Konovalov, who once operated on me, temporarily arranged for my works to be stored in the hospital basement.

It looks like your work was always met with understanding. Or is that not the case?

I can tell you this: the same painting can make a completely different impression on different people, even on professionals. For example, there is one famous fine arts expert, Elena Murina, who once proclaimed my painting 'The White Tree' to be a masterpiece. But after examining the very same painting, the department head of the Pushkin Museum asked me just one question: 'What is that puddle under the mountain you have over there?'

Were you ever tempted to move to the West?

No, never. First of all, I know nothing when it comes to languages. To the same extent that my father had a knack for languages – he knew six foreign languages – I am hopeless when it comes to them.

Nevertheless, you still once had a personal exhibition in New York.

This was also one of the lucky coincidences in my life, when they put together the various privately owned works that were being held in the United States. So they made an exhibition out of these works. Unfortunately, I wasn't able to attend personally because I didn't have a visa.

What gives you motivation to work?

I think that love for a woman determines a lot in life.

People usually think of artists as flighty people. Do you agree?

Personally, I am not a flighty person. Just the opposite. I have always fallen in love deeply and for very long periods of time. Like many artists, I frequently painted my wife. Perhaps she was not a blinding beauty, but she had a very willowy figure and it was a pleasure for me to paint her.

On several occasions in life, Leo Tolstoy grew cold towards his wife only to fall in love with her all over again. Has that ever happened to you?

No, I never lost my feelings for Inga. When she died of cancer, at one point it seemed that my soul had died with her. Then, thankfully, my second wife, Olga, appeared. I owe so much to her. She is a doctor at the neurosurgery Institute where I was a patient. At the time, I didn't want to let anyone into my life. I was afraid to do so. But Olga was the only person who not only managed to pull me out of my depression, but also to find a common language with my son Nikolai.

However, the years are flying by, and I recently read an interesting phrase: 'When your love for a woman disappears, it is time to start loving nature'.

And is it already time for you to start loving nature?

Yes, perhaps it is. Unfortunately.
Interviewed by Vera Medvedeva

Also available from Spokesman

THIS I CANNOT FORGET
The Memoirs of Nikolai Bukharin's Widow
By ANNA LARINA

'I lived with Nikolai Ivanovich Bukharin, my husband, through what were both the happiest and the most exciting days of our lives. But our last six months together were made so difficult, so painful, that each day felt like a century. This memoir of that time was written over the many years since, set down in fragments whenever I found relief from family worries and cares ... You must understand that, from childhood, I lived among people who were totally dedicated to the cause of socialist revolution.'

From the author's Preface

ISBN 978 0 85124 7816 £19.95 410 pages illustrated

* * *

THE CASE OF NIKOLAI BUKHARIN
by KEN COATES

Published in 1978 in support of the long-term campaign for Bukharin's rehabilitation, which was eventually to achieve success a decade later, this little book shows how the indictment made against him in 1938, in the third of Stalin's show trials, had already completely crumbled away. The evidence presented includes important documents on the struggle of the Bukharin family for the good name of their most famous relative. It has been translated and published in China in an edition of tens of thousands of copies.

ISBN: 978 0 85124 241 5   £4.95 Paperback

* * *

SELECTED WRITINGS ON THE STATE AND THE TRANSITION TO SOCIALISM
By N I BUKHARIN

Edited by Richard B Day
Foreword by Stephen F Cohen
ISBN:978 0 85124 275 0   £20.00 Hardback

www.spokesmanbooks.com

Stalin and Bukharin muster on top of Lenin's Mausoleum in October 1929, a month before Bukharin was expelled from the Politburo. (Credit: David King)